TABLE OF CONTENTS

INTRODUCTION

The workplace is undergoing a seismic shift. The traditional nine-to-five office setup, once considered the gold standard of professional life, is evolving into a dynamic, flexible ecosystem where remote and hybrid work models are taking center stage. This change, accelerated by the global pandemic and sustained by technological advancements, is redefining how we work, where we work, and even why we work.

But what does this future hold for you? How can you thrive in a world where the office may no longer be a fixed location, and success depends as much on adaptability as it does on expertise? These are the questions this eBook seeks to answer.

Whether you're a seasoned professional seeking to enhance your remote work skills, a recent graduate embarking on your career journey, or a business leader navigating the complexities of managing a hybrid workforce, this guide will provide valuable insights and actionable advice.

Let's explore,

- **The Rise of Remote and Hybrid Work:** Understanding the forces driving this transformation, from technological advancements to changing employee expectations.

- **Building a Successful Remote Work Foundation:** Essential tips for creating an effective home office, cultivating a productive work routine, and maintaining focus and motivation.

- **Mastering Communication and Collaboration:** Strategies for effective communication and collaboration within remote and hybrid teams, including best practices for virtual meetings, project management tools, and building strong relationships.

- **Navigating the Challenges of Remote Work:** Addressing common challenges such as loneliness, isolation, and maintaining work-life balance.

- **The Future of Work: Trends and Predictions:** Exploring the emerging trends shaping the future of work, such as AI, automation, and the gig economy.

- **Preparing for the Future: Developing Essential Skills:** Identifying and developing the skills and competencies that will be most valuable in the future of work, such as digital literacy, critical thinking, and adaptability.

This ebook is your roadmap to success in the evolving world of work. By embracing the opportunities and navigating the challenges of remote and hybrid careers, you can unlock new levels of flexibility, fulfillment, and professional growth.

Why the Future of Work Matters

The way we work has profound implications for individuals, businesses, and society at large. For individuals, remote and hybrid work offers unprecedented flexibility but also introduces challenges like isolation, blurred boundaries between personal and professional life, and the need for constant upskilling. For businesses, these models promise cost savings and access to a global talent pool but require new strategies for team management and collaboration. For society, the shift is reshaping urban landscapes, commuting patterns, and even cultural norms.

The hybrid and remote work models are not just trends; they are here to stay. A 2025 study by leading labor analysts predicts that over 60% of knowledge workers will operate in hybrid settings, while fully remote roles will remain a staple in industries like technology, media, and consulting. Understanding these shifts is no longer optional—it's essential for staying relevant and competitive.

Who Is This Book For?

Whether you're an employee navigating the transition to remote work, a manager adapting to leading a dispersed team, or an entrepreneur building a business in the digital era, this book is for you. It's designed to equip you with the tools, strategies, and insights needed to excel in a remote or hybrid work environment.

If you're wondering how to:

- Set up a productive home office,
- Land a remote or hybrid job,
- Balance work and life without burnout, or
- Lead a high-performing remote team,

then you've come to the right place.

What This Book Covers

This eBook takes a comprehensive approach, guiding you through every facet of remote and hybrid work. Here's a sneak peek at what you'll learn:

1. **The Foundations**: Understand the evolution of work and the key drivers behind the remote and hybrid trends.

2. **Practical Strategies**: Discover actionable tips for setting up your workspace, mastering time management, and maintaining strong professional relationships, even from afar.

3. **Leadership Insights**: Learn how to effectively manage and lead remote teams, fostering engagement, trust, and productivity.

4. **Overcoming Challenges**: Tackle common issues like isolation, technology fatigue, and communication barriers with proven strategies.

5. **Future-Forward Thinking**: Prepare for the next big shifts in the workplace by staying ahead of emerging trends and technology.

Each chapter is packed with practical advice, real-world examples, and expert insights to ensure you're not just surviving the future of work but thriving in it.

Why This eBook Stands Out

Unlike generic guides, this book is tailored to the realities of 2025 and beyond. It addresses not only the "how" but also the "why" of remote and hybrid work. By blending actionable steps with forward-looking perspectives, it equips you with the knowledge to adapt today and anticipate tomorrow. Think of this book as your personal mentor, providing clarity and confidence in a world of constant change.

How to Use This Book

The structure of this book is designed to be both flexible and comprehensive. You can read it cover to cover or jump to sections that resonate with your immediate needs. Each chapter includes actionable takeaways, making it easy to apply what you've learned right away.

A World of Opportunities Awaits

The future of work isn't something to fear—it's an opportunity to reimagine your career on your terms. Remote and hybrid work offers the flexibility to craft a lifestyle that aligns with your goals, values, and aspirations. With the right mindset, skills, and strategies, you can turn this new era into your greatest advantage.

Let's embark on this journey together. By the end of this book, you'll not only understand the future of work—you'll be ready to own it.

Chapter 1: The Evolution of Work

The concept of "work" has evolved significantly over the past few centuries. From the Industrial Revolution to the Digital Age, how we earn a living and interact with our professional environments has shifted dramatically. The 21st century, in particular, has seen a rapid transformation in work culture, driven by technology, globalization, and societal shifts. This chapter explores the historical trajectory of work, the rise of remote and hybrid models, and the critical factors influencing these changes.

1.1 The Historical Context of Work

From Agrarian to Industrial Economies

For much of human history, work revolved around agriculture. Families worked on farms, and livelihoods depended on local economies. However, the Industrial Revolution in the 18th and 19th centuries marked a turning point. Factories sprang up, urbanization surged, and work shifted from fields to assembly lines.

- **Work as Location-Based**: The industrial model tied work to specific locations, such as factories and offices.
- **Structured Work Hours**: The concept of fixed work hours emerged, giving rise to the standard "nine-to-five" schedule.

The Information Age

The late 20th century ushered in the Information Age, characterized by the rise of computers, the internet, and telecommunications. This era transformed work yet again:

- **Knowledge Work Emerges**: Jobs became more focused on information processing rather than physical labor.
- **Globalization**: Advances in communication technology allowed companies to expand operations globally, creating a demand for cross-border collaboration.

1.2 The Rise of Remote Work

The Remote Work Experiment

While remote work existed in niche forms before 2020, it gained mainstream attention during the COVID-19 pandemic. Forced lockdowns acted as a global experiment in remote work, pushing companies to adapt overnight.

- **Technological Enablers**: Tools like Zoom, Microsoft Teams, and Slack became lifelines for organizations.
- **Breaking Location Barriers**: Employees proved they could be as productive at home as in the office, challenging traditional assumptions.

Post-Pandemic Persistence

As restrictions eased, remote work didn't disappear. Instead, it became a preferred option for many workers and businesses.

- **Employee Demand**: Surveys show that a significant percentage of employees prefer flexibility over rigid office structures.

- **Business Benefits**: Companies realized cost savings from reduced office space and access to a broader talent pool.

1.3 What is Hybrid Work?

Definition and Key Features

Hybrid work is a model that combines elements of remote and on-site work. Employees split their time between working from home and working in an office or another centralized location.

- **Flexible Schedules**: Hybrid work often allows employees to choose when and where they work.

- **Collaborative Focus**: Offices are increasingly used for team collaboration rather than individual tasks.

Benefits of Hybrid Work

- **Work-Life Balance**: Employees can better manage personal and professional responsibilities.

- **Increased Productivity**: Workers can focus on tasks at home and collaborate in person as needed.

- **Attracting Talent**: Hybrid models appeal to younger generations entering the workforce.

1.4 Key Drivers of Change

Technological Advancements

Technology has been the backbone of the remote and hybrid work revolution. Key developments include:

- **High-Speed Internet**: Broadband and 5G networks have made remote work feasible in most parts of the world.

- **Cloud Computing**: Tools like Google Workspace and Microsoft 365 allow seamless access to work files from anywhere.

- **Collaboration Platforms**: Software like Trello, Asana, and Slack enable teams to stay connected and aligned.

Globalization and Talent Pools

Globalization has pushed organizations to rethink how they operate:

- **Access to Global Talent**: Remote work allows companies to hire the best talent, regardless of location.

- **Cultural Exchange**: Diverse teams bring fresh perspectives, fostering innovation and creativity.

Societal Shifts

Changing attitudes toward work-life balance, mental health, and job satisfaction have also driven the move toward flexible work models.

- **Work-Life Integration**: Employees now value roles that offer flexibility and purpose.

- **Millennial and Gen Z Influence**: Younger generations prioritize flexibility and opportunities for growth over traditional job perks.

1.5 Challenges in the Transition

While the shift to remote and hybrid work has been transformative, it hasn't been without challenges:

- **Technology Gaps**: Not all employees have access to the tools or reliable internet required for remote work.

- **Isolation**: Remote workers can struggle with feelings of disconnection and loneliness.

- **Management Adjustments**: Leaders must learn new ways to measure productivity and foster team cohesion.

1.6 The Road Ahead

The evolution of work is far from over. As technology advances and societal expectations shift, we can expect even more changes. Predictions for the future include:

- **AI Integration**: Artificial intelligence will continue to automate tasks, requiring workers to upskill regularly.

- **Redefinition of Offices**: Offices will transform into hubs for collaboration and innovation rather than daily workspaces.

- **Sustainability**: Companies will incorporate eco-friendly practices into work arrangements, including reducing the carbon footprint of commuting.

The evolution of work has been shaped by technological, societal, and economic forces. Understanding this trajectory is crucial for navigating the future. Remote and hybrid work models are not fleeting trends—they are the foundation of tomorrow's workplace. As you move forward, embracing flexibility, adaptability, and continuous learning will be key to thriving in this new era.

Chapter 2: Building a Remote or Hybrid Career

Remote and hybrid work offer immense opportunities for flexibility, autonomy, and global collaboration. However, succeeding in this new environment requires identifying the right roles, acquiring the necessary skills, and mastering the application process. This section provides a detailed roadmap to help you build a rewarding remote or hybrid career.

H1: Finding the Right Role

Identifying the perfect role in a remote or hybrid setup requires a strategic approach. It's not just about finding a job that pays well—it's about finding one that aligns with your skills, interests, and work-life balance preferences.

H2: Skills in Demand for Remote and Hybrid Jobs

Remote and hybrid jobs often demand a blend of technical, creative, and soft skills. Employers prioritize candidates who can thrive independently and contribute effectively to a dispersed team.

Technical, Creative, and Soft Skills

1. **Technical Skills**

   - Digital Proficiency: Master tools like Slack, Zoom, Trello, and Google Workspace to streamline communication and collaboration.

   - Data Analysis: Skills in Excel, SQL, Python, or Power BI are valuable in roles requiring data-driven decisions.

   - Cybersecurity Awareness: Knowledge of online safety practices is vital for protecting sensitive information in remote work setups.

2. **Creative Skills**

   - Content Creation: Writing, graphic design, and video editing are critical in marketing, branding, and online media roles.

   - Problem-Solving: Creativity is essential for developing innovative solutions to remote work challenges.

3. **Soft Skills**

   - Communication: Strong written and verbal communication skills are crucial in environments where face-to-face interaction is limited.

   - Time Management: Ability to prioritize tasks and meet deadlines without constant supervision.

   - Adaptability: Flexibility to adjust to changing technologies and workflows.

Upskilling and Continuous Learning

The fast-paced nature of remote and hybrid work means staying current is non-negotiable.

- Take Online Courses: Platforms like Coursera, Udemy, and edX offer affordable certifications in tech, business, and creative fields.

- Attend Virtual Workshops: Participate in webinars and conferences to learn from industry experts.

- Set Learning Goals: Dedicate time each week to improving a skill, whether it's coding, public speaking, or mastering a new software.

Where to Look for Opportunities

Finding remote and hybrid jobs requires exploring dedicated platforms and leveraging personal connections in the digital space.

H3: Remote Job Boards and Platforms

1. **Popular Platforms:**

   - Remote.co: Offers listings tailored to remote roles across various industries.

   - We Work Remotely: Focuses on jobs in development, design, sales, and customer support.

   - AngelList: Great for finding remote roles in startups.

   - Upwork and Fiverr: Ideal for freelancers and gig workers looking for project-based work.

2. **Company Websites:** Many companies post remote opportunities directly on their careers page. Use targeted searches to find these listings.

3. **Social Media**: Follow hashtags like #RemoteWork, #HybridJobs, and #WorkFromHome on platforms like LinkedIn and Twitter to discover new openings.

Networking in the Digital Age

Networking is as critical for remote roles as it is for traditional jobs—but the approach differs.

- LinkedIn Connections: Use LinkedIn to connect with professionals in your industry, engage with their posts, and share relevant content to build your presence.

- Virtual Communities: Join online forums, Slack groups, or Facebook groups centered around remote work and specific industries.

- Online Events: Attend virtual career fairs, webinars, and networking meetups to make meaningful connections.

H1: Landing the Job

Securing a remote or hybrid role requires crafting a standout application and excelling in virtual interviews.

Crafting an Impressive Digital Resume

A digital resume for remote roles should emphasize your ability to work independently and your familiarity with relevant tools.

- **Highlight Remote Work Skills**: Include experience with virtual tools and platforms. Mention soft skills like communication and self-discipline.

- **Use Metrics: Showcase achievements with quantifiable results.** For example: "Increased remote team productivity by 25% through improved communication workflows."

- **Tailor for Each Role:** Customize your resume to align with the specific job description and requirements.

- **Professional Design:** Use online resume builders like Canva or Zety to create visually appealing, easy-to-read resumes.

Nailing Virtual Interviews

Virtual interviews have become the norm for remote and hybrid jobs. Preparation and presentation are key to making a strong impression.

Preparing Your Setup and Presentation

1. **Technical Preparation:**

   - Test your internet connection and ensure it's stable.

   - Use a reliable webcam and microphone.

   - Familiarize yourself with the video conferencing platform (e.g., Zoom, Google Meet).

2. **Environment:**

   - Choose a quiet, well-lit space free from distractions.

   - Ensure your background is tidy or use a virtual background that looks professional.

3. **Dress the Part:**

   - Dress professionally, even if the interview is remote. It shows respect for the interviewer and the opportunity.

4. **Body Language:**

   - Maintain good posture, make eye contact with the camera, and use hand gestures naturally.

Common Questions and How to Answer Them

1. **"How do you manage your time when working remotely?"**

   - Example Answer: "I use tools like Trello to prioritize tasks and the Pomodoro Technique to stay focused. I also set boundaries between work and personal life to avoid burnout."

2. **"Describe a time you solved a problem while working remotely."**

   - Example Answer: "In my previous role, a miscommunication led to a project delay. I organized a quick Zoom call, clarified tasks, and created a shared checklist to keep everyone aligned."

3. **"What tools and platforms are you familiar with?"**

   - Example Answer: "I've extensively used Slack, Asana, and Zoom for collaboration, and I'm proficient in Google Workspace for document management."

4. **"How do you handle communication challenges in a remote setting?"**

   - Example Answer: "I ensure clear communication by using concise emails, regular video check-ins, and shared documents to track progress."

Notes: Building a remote or hybrid career involves strategic planning, continuous learning, and effective self-presentation. By honing the right skills, exploring the best platforms, and excelling in virtual interviews, you can position yourself as a top candidate in the competitive job market of 2025 and beyond.

Chapter 3: Thriving in Remote and Hybrid Work Environments

Once you've secured a remote or hybrid job, the next challenge is excelling in the role. This part focuses on strategies to maintain productivity, foster connections, and achieve work-life balance in these unique work environments.

H1: Staying Productive

Designing an Optimal Workspace

- **Ergonomics Matter**: Invest in a comfortable chair and desk to support long hours of work.
- **Minimize Distractions**: Choose a quiet location and reduce visual clutter to enhance focus.
- **Lighting and Comfort**: Use natural light where possible and ensure your workspace is well-lit to avoid strain.

Managing Your Time Effectively

- **Set a Schedule**: Establish clear working hours and stick to them.
- **Use Productivity Tools**: Apps like Todoist, Trello, and Notion help track tasks and priorities.
- **Batch Similar Tasks**: Grouping similar tasks together can help maintain focus and efficiency.

Avoiding Burnout

- **Take Breaks**: Use techniques like the Pomodoro Technique to incorporate regular breaks.
- **Set Boundaries**: Communicate your availability to family, friends, and colleagues to avoid interruptions.
- **Practice Self-Care**: Exercise, meditate, and maintain hobbies outside of work.

H2: Building Strong Remote Relationships

Effective Communication

- **Proactive Updates**: Keep your team informed about your progress and challenges.
- **Use Multiple Channels**: Adapt communication styles depending on the situation—email for detailed discussions, chat for quick updates, and video calls for important topics.
- **Clarity is Key**: Avoid misunderstandings by being concise and clear in your messages.

Collaboration in Distributed Teams

- **Virtual Meetings**: Prepare agendas, stick to time limits, and actively engage during calls.
- **Shared Tools**: Utilize platforms like Google Workspace, Monday.com, or Jira for seamless collaboration.
- **Celebrate Milestones**: Acknowledge team achievements to foster morale and camaraderie.

Cultural Sensitivity in Global Teams

- **Be Inclusive**: Respect cultural differences and time zone constraints.
- **Learn About Colleagues**: Understanding their customs and work preferences builds stronger relationships.

H3: Achieving Work-Life Balance

Separating Work and Personal Life

- **Create Physical Boundaries**: If possible, work in a space separate from your living area.
- **End-of-Day Rituals**: Develop habits like shutting down your laptop and taking a walk to signal the end of the workday.

Leveraging Flexibility

- **Adapt to Your Peak Hours**: Work during the times you feel most productive.
- **Personal Time**: Use the flexibility of remote work to prioritize family and personal activities.

Staying Connected Socially

- **Virtual Social Events**: Participate in online team-building activities or casual video calls.
- **Local Networking**: Join coworking spaces or attend meetups to interact with professionals in your area.

Chapter 4: Overcoming Challenges in Remote and Hybrid Work

Remote and hybrid work offer numerous benefits, but they also come with challenges. This part addresses common obstacles and provides strategies to overcome them effectively.

H1: Addressing Isolation

Staying Connected with Team Members

- **Regular Check-Ins**: Schedule one-on-one or team calls to maintain connections.
- **Informal Chats**: Engage in non-work-related conversations to build rapport.

Building a Support Network

- **Online Communities**: Join forums or social media groups dedicated to remote workers.
- **Professional Mentors**: Seek advice and guidance from experienced professionals.

H2: Managing Distractions

Household Interruptions

- **Set Expectations**: Communicate your work hours to family members or roommates.
- **Create a Routine**: Build a daily schedule to align personal and professional responsibilities.

Digital Distractions

- **Use Focus Tools**: Applications like Freedom or Focus@Will help block distracting websites.
- **Limit Notifications**: Turn off non-essential alerts on your devices during work hours.

H3: Handling Performance and Accountability

Setting Goals

- **Use SMART Goals**: Specific, Measurable, Achievable, Relevant, and Time-bound goals help track progress.
- **Frequent Reviews**: Regularly assess your achievements and adjust plans as needed.

Measuring Productivity

- **Task Tracking**: Tools like Asana or ClickUp provide insights into task completion and deadlines.
- **Performance Metrics**: Align your KPIs (Key Performance Indicators) with team or organizational goals.

H4: Balancing Hybrid Work Models

Transitioning Between Home and Office

- **Plan Ahead**: Organize tasks based on where you'll be working—creative tasks at home, collaborative tasks at the office.
- **Stay Organized**: Maintain a portable system (e.g., a digital planner) for seamless transitions.

Ensuring Fairness in Hybrid Teams

- **Equal Opportunities**: Encourage equal participation in meetings and decision-making for remote and in-office employees.
- **Transparent Communication**: Share updates consistently to keep everyone informed.

H5: Adapting to Change

Embracing Technological Advances

- **Stay Updated**: Regularly learn about new tools and platforms that improve productivity.

- **Adopt Early**: Be open to experimenting with emerging technologies like VR for meetings or AI for task automation.

Coping with Industry Changes

- **Be Flexible**: Adapt to changes in organizational policies or market demands.

- **Develop Resilience**: Maintain a positive attitude and seek solutions to challenges.

Notes: Thriving in remote and hybrid work environments requires more than technical skills—it demands discipline, adaptability, and proactive communication. By addressing challenges like isolation, distractions, and accountability, you can build a fulfilling career that leverages the flexibility and opportunities these work models provide.

Chapter 5: Overcoming Challenges in Remote and Hybrid Work

Remote and hybrid work environments provide flexibility and convenience, but they also present unique challenges. From combating isolation to managing technology overload and resolving conflicts, this section provides detailed strategies to tackle these issues effectively and maintain a healthy, productive work experience.

H1: Tackling Isolation and Burnout

One of the most common challenges of remote work is feeling isolated from colleagues and work culture, which can contribute to burnout. Addressing these concerns is crucial for long-term success.

Recognizing the Signs

Understanding the early indicators of isolation and burnout helps in taking preventive measures:

- **Emotional Signs**: Feelings of loneliness, frustration, or lack of motivation.

- **Behavioral Changes**: Reduced productivity, procrastination, or avoiding communication.

- **Physical Symptoms**: Fatigue, headaches, or trouble sleeping, often linked to stress.

Being self-aware and identifying these signs can enable you to act before the situation worsens.

Strategies for Mental Well-Being

1. **Foster Social Connections**:
   - Engage in casual conversations with colleagues over messaging platforms or during virtual meetings.
   - Join professional communities and attend virtual or in-person meetups.

2. **Schedule "Me Time"**:
   - Dedicate time daily for activities you enjoy, such as reading, exercising, or hobbies.
   - Practice mindfulness through meditation or breathing exercises to manage stress.

3. **Set Boundaries**:
   - Clearly define work hours and personal time to prevent work from encroaching on your personal life.
   - Communicate these boundaries to colleagues and family members.

4. **Seek Professional Support**:
   - Don't hesitate to consult a mental health professional if feelings of burnout persist.
   - Utilize employee assistance programs or counseling services if available.

H2: Navigating Technology Overload

While technology enables remote work, excessive reliance on digital tools can lead to fatigue and inefficiency. Managing your tech usage is essential to avoid becoming overwhelmed.

Avoiding "Zoom Fatigue"

Video meetings, while necessary, can be mentally exhausting when overused. To combat "Zoom fatigue," consider the following:

- **Limit Meeting Frequency**: Reduce unnecessary meetings and consolidate topics into fewer, more effective sessions.
- **Take Breaks**: Schedule buffer periods between meetings to rest your eyes and mind.
- **Use Audio When Possible**: Switch off the video feature during less formal discussions to reduce screen strain.
- **Optimize Meeting Length**: Keep meetings concise and to the point by using clear agendas and action plans.

Streamlining Tools and Processes

The abundance of digital tools can sometimes complicate workflows. Simplify by:

- **Choosing the Right Tools**: Select platforms that integrate seamlessly, like Slack for communication and Asana for task management.
- **Consolidating Functions**: Use multipurpose tools that handle various tasks instead of juggling several single-function apps.
- **Training and Adaptation**: Invest time in learning the full potential of your tools to maximize efficiency.

H1: Handling Conflict and Miscommunication

Conflict is inevitable, even in virtual settings. Miscommunication, cultural differences, or unclear expectations can lead to disagreements. Handling such issues promptly and effectively is key to maintaining a harmonious work environment.

Addressing Issues Early

Proactive conflict management minimizes misunderstandings and prevents small issues from escalating:

- **Encourage Open Communication**: Create a safe environment for team members to voice concerns or feedback without fear of judgment.
- **Clarify Expectations**: Ensure all team members understand their roles, responsibilities, and deadlines to avoid confusion.
- **Monitor Team Dynamics**: Be attentive to signs of tension or disengagement during virtual meetings or communications.

Best Practices for Conflict Resolution

1. **Acknowledge the Problem**:
   - Begin by recognizing that an issue exists and inviting all parties involved to share their perspectives.

2. **Maintain Neutrality**:
   - Approach conflicts with an open mind and avoid assigning blame prematurely. Focus on facts rather than emotions.

3. **Use Clear and Empathetic Communication**:
   - Listen actively to all sides, repeat key points to ensure understanding, and express empathy toward others' feelings.

4. **Focus on Solutions**:

   ▪ Work collaboratively to identify actionable steps that address the root cause of the conflict.

5. **Document Resolutions**:

   ▪ Record agreements or changes to ensure everyone is aligned moving forward.

6. **Seek Mediation if Necessary**:

   ▪ If conflicts persist, involve a neutral third party, such as an HR representative or team leader, to mediate discussions.

Overcoming challenges in remote and hybrid work environments is critical to sustaining long-term productivity and job satisfaction. By proactively addressing isolation and burnout, managing technology use, and resolving conflicts effectively, you can create a more balanced and successful work experience. These strategies not only improve your professional life but also enhance your overall well-being, ensuring that remote or hybrid work remains a viable and fulfilling option for years to come.

Chapter 6: The Future Beyond 2025

As the workplace continues to evolve, new trends, technologies, and challenges will shape the way we work. Looking beyond 2025, the dynamics of remote and hybrid careers will be influenced by several key factors, including artificial intelligence (AI), globalization, and the need for continuous learning. This section explores predictions for the workplace of tomorrow and how individuals can prepare for the next big shift in their careers.

H1: Predictions for the Workplace of Tomorrow

The workplace will continue to be shaped by advancements in technology, shifting global dynamics, and the changing demands of employees and employers. Below are some key predictions for the workplace of the future:

The Role of Artificial Intelligence and Automation

AI and Automation Will Revolutionize Jobs:

- **Job Transformation**: By 2025 and beyond, AI and automation will be integrated into almost every aspect of work. While some jobs may disappear, many will evolve to require new skills. Routine tasks, like data entry or basic customer service, will be automated, allowing employees to focus on higher-value work that requires creativity and decision-making.

- **AI-Enhanced Roles**: Rather than replacing jobs entirely, AI will augment the roles of human workers. For example, AI can assist doctors with diagnosing diseases, help marketers optimize campaigns, or aid financial analysts in identifying trends. This trend will lead to more specialized roles that blend technical skills with human judgment.

- **New Career Paths**: As AI and automation evolve, entirely new fields will emerge. Roles like AI ethicists, data trainers, or automation specialists will become more common. Individuals who stay updated on advancements in AI will have a competitive advantage in the workforce.

Increased Use of Virtual Assistants:

- As technology becomes smarter, virtual assistants like Siri, Alexa, or custom-built AI tools will play an even greater role in the workplace, managing tasks, scheduling meetings, and organizing data. This integration will streamline work processes and make employees more efficient.

- **Smart Workspaces**: The workplace will likely see a rise in smart environments—offices equipped with AI systems that learn and adapt to workers' preferences. These environments will adjust lighting, temperature, and even suggest personalized work breaks based on individual needs.

The Impact of Globalization on Careers
A More Interconnected World:

- **Global Workforce Expansion**: The rise of remote work, combined with globalization, will result in a highly interconnected workforce. Professionals will work alongside colleagues from around the world, benefiting from diverse perspectives, skills, and experiences. This trend will encourage cross-cultural collaboration and exchange of ideas.

- **Increased Competition**: While this interconnectedness opens up more career opportunities, it also means individuals will face more competition. Workers from countries with lower living costs will compete with those in high-income regions, potentially driving down wages in some industries.

- **Global Career Mobility**: Remote work and flexible job arrangements will make it easier for people to work in different countries without leaving their homes. Professionals will have more opportunities to pursue international careers without physically relocating, which may lead to a more diverse workforce that transcends borders.

Localization of Work:

- Despite globalization, companies will continue to focus on localizing products and services to cater to specific markets. This trend will create jobs that require deep knowledge of local cultures, regulations, and preferences, while still benefiting from a global work network.

- **Cross-Border Collaboration**: Hybrid work arrangements will allow companies to set up virtual teams that can work across time zones, giving them access to global talent pools. This will make it easier for businesses to hire the best candidates for the job, regardless of location.

H1: Preparing for the Next Big Shift

The rapid changes in the workplace will require workers to be adaptable, agile, and forward-thinking. Here are strategies for preparing for the evolving career landscape beyond 2025:

Lifelong Learning as a Key to Success

Continuous Skill Development:

- **Adapting to Technological Changes**: As new tools and technologies emerge; workers must remain committed to continuous learning. Lifelong learning will become essential for staying relevant in an increasingly automated and AI-driven world.

- **Specialization and Upskilling**: Professionals will need to focus on gaining deep expertise in their chosen fields while staying up to date with emerging trends. Upskilling will involve learning new technical skills, such as data science, coding, and AI, as well as soft skills like creativity, problem-solving, and leadership.

- **Self-Directed Learning**: With the increasing availability of online courses, certifications, and resources, individuals can take charge of their learning journey. Websites like Coursera, Udemy, and LinkedIn Learning will continue to offer opportunities for workers to build the skills they need to succeed in the future workplace.

Resilience and Adaptability:

- To thrive in an environment of constant change, workers must develop resilience and adaptability. This means embracing new tools, learning new methods of working, and being open to feedback. The ability to pivot quickly and remain agile will be key to navigating the unpredictable future.

Embracing Change and Uncertainty

Mindset Shift:

- **Thriving in Uncertainty**: The future will bring both challenges and opportunities. Workers who embrace change and uncertainty will be better equipped to handle transitions. Developing a growth mindset—where challenges are viewed as opportunities for growth—will be essential.

- **Accepting Risk and Experimentation**: The future of work will require a willingness to experiment with new approaches, tools, and roles. Professionals who can step out of their comfort zone and take calculated risks will gain a competitive edge.

Personalized Career Paths:

- **Job Customization**: As remote and hybrid work become the norm, workers will have more flexibility in shaping their careers. They will be able to pursue diverse roles or create portfolios of work that blend multiple interests. This will provide workers with more autonomy over their professional paths, enabling them to align their careers with their personal goals and values.

- **Gig Economy Growth**: The gig economy will continue to expand, offering professionals the opportunity to work on short-term projects, freelance, or consult. Workers will be able to pursue multiple income streams while maintaining the flexibility to adapt to changes in the job market.

Notes: The future beyond 2025 holds immense potential and exciting possibilities. As technology continues to reshape the workplace, professionals will need to adapt to a rapidly changing environment. Embracing the role of AI and automation, staying globally connected, and committing to lifelong learning will be the keys to success. By preparing for these shifts and remaining open to change, individuals can thrive in the evolving world of work, creating fulfilling careers that are both sustainable and aligned with the needs of the future.

Chapter 7: Wrapping Up

The future of work is unfolding before our eyes, and it presents opportunities and challenges that will reshape careers in profound ways. The shift towards remote and hybrid work models, the rise of artificial intelligence and automation, and the growing importance of continuous learning are just the beginning. The future workplace will demand greater adaptability, resilience, and a willingness to embrace new technologies and ways of working.

As we navigate the complexities of the evolving work environment, it's essential to understand that change is inevitable, but how we prepare for it can make all the difference. This guide has provided you with the tools, strategies, and insights to stay ahead of the curve and thrive in an ever-changing landscape.

Key Takeaways

1. **Remote and Hybrid Work is Here to Stay**:
   - The global shift towards flexible work models is not a passing trend. Remote and hybrid work arrangements will continue to evolve and offer individuals the flexibility to design their careers around their personal and professional goals.

2. **Embrace Technological Advancements**:
   - Artificial intelligence, automation, and digital tools will reshape industries, making certain tasks obsolete while creating new roles and opportunities. Understanding and adopting these technologies will be crucial for staying relevant in the future workforce.

3. **Lifelong Learning is Essential**:
   - The future workplace will place a premium on those who commit to continuous upskilling. Whether through formal education or self-directed learning, developing both technical and soft skills will be key to career longevity.

4. **Globalization Creates Opportunities and Challenges**:
   - As the world becomes more interconnected, competition will increase, but so will access to diverse opportunities. Global collaboration will be a defining feature of future work environments, providing access to international networks and cross-cultural experiences.

5. **Mental Health and Well-Being are Non-Negotiable**:
   - Remote and hybrid work environments can lead to isolation, burnout, and stress. It's crucial to prioritize mental well-being by setting boundaries, seeking social connections, and maintaining a healthy work-life balance.

Your Action Plan for Navigating the Future of Work

The future of work is not something you simply react to—it's something you proactively shape. To ensure that you're prepared for the shifts that are coming, here's your step-by-step action plan to successfully navigate the future of work:

1. Embrace the Digital Revolution

Up-skill and Re-skill:

- Identify the skills that are in demand in your industry—whether it's AI, data science, or digital marketing. Use online platforms like Coursera, LinkedIn Learning, and Udemy to start acquiring these skills.

- Take specialized courses to stay ahead of trends, and always be open to learning something new, whether it's a new software, communication tool, or a skill that helps you work more effectively.

Adopt Technology:

- Stay current with the latest digital tools and technologies that streamline remote work. Invest in software that improves productivity and collaboration, such as project management tools (e.g., Asana, Trello) or communication platforms (e.g., Slack, Microsoft Teams).

2. Prioritize Mental Health and Well-Being

Set Healthy Boundaries:

- Create a structured daily routine and clearly define your work hours. Resist the temptation to work outside these boundaries, especially when working remotely or in a hybrid arrangement.

Foster Social Connections:

- Make time for virtual coffee breaks or in-person social activities with colleagues. Building a strong network of professional and personal connections will keep you engaged and prevent feelings of isolation.

Practice Self-Care:

- Prioritize activities that keep you grounded, whether it's exercise, meditation, hobbies, or quality time with loved ones. Implement stress-relief strategies like breathing exercises or mindfulness techniques to recharge.

3. Build a Personal Brand and Network

Create a Strong Online Presence:

- Cultivate your professional online brand by regularly updating your LinkedIn profile, writing articles, and sharing insights on industry trends. By positioning yourself as a thought leader, you'll stay top of mind for recruiters and colleagues.

Expand Your Network:

- Actively engage in virtual events, webinars, and networking groups. By participating in global communities, you increase your chances of finding new opportunities and forming strategic connections.

4. Stay Agile and Be Open to Change

Develop a Growth Mindset:

- In an era of constant change, the most successful individuals are those who view challenges as opportunities for growth. Be open to trying new things, whether it's a different career path, remote work environment, or a new role that requires you to learn new skills.

Experiment with New Roles and Projects:

- Take on side projects or freelance gigs that align with your long-term goals. These experiences will help you explore new fields, diversify your skill set, and make you more adaptable to changes in the job market.

5. Prepare for the Global Workforce

Learn Cross-Cultural Communication:

- As globalization increases, you will likely work with colleagues from around the world. Strengthen your ability to communicate across cultures by learning about different work styles, etiquette, and communication preferences. This will enhance your collaboration in diverse teams.

Stay Informed on Global Trends:

- Stay updated on trends and shifts happening globally, such as economic changes, geopolitical developments, or advancements in industries like AI, healthcare, and sustainability. A broad understanding of the global landscape will give you an edge in your career.

6. Be a Champion of Innovation and Change

Adopt a Forward-Thinking Approach:

- Constantly challenge yourself to think about how you can contribute to innovation within your field. Whether you're in a technical, creative, or managerial role, keep asking, "What's next?" and "How can I improve processes, tools, or practices?"

Lead by Example:

- Be a role model for embracing change and technology. Encourage your colleagues and teams to explore new ways of working, and foster a culture of adaptability and experimentation.

Notes: As we look toward the future of work, the key to success lies in embracing the opportunities ahead with a proactive mindset. The ability to navigate technological advancements, stay connected in a global workforce, prioritize well-being, and continuously adapt to change will be the differentiators between those who thrive and those who struggle. By taking action today to build new skills, foster meaningful relationships, and stay flexible in the face of uncertainty, you'll be well-equipped to shape your career and thrive in the workplace of tomorrow.

Appendices

As you continue to navigate the world of remote and hybrid work, it's important to equip yourself with the right resources, tools, and strategies. This section offers valuable resources for remote and hybrid workers, including job boards, platforms, and productivity tools. Additionally, sample templates for job applications and productivity schedules are provided to streamline your work processes.

H1: Resources for Remote and Hybrid Workers

There are numerous resources available to support remote and hybrid workers in their quest for career success. From job boards to specialized tools for communication and collaboration, these resources can help you find opportunities, stay productive, and effectively manage your career. Here are some of the most important ones:

Job Boards, Tools, and Platforms

The rise of remote and hybrid work has led to the creation of specialized platforms designed to connect job seekers with employers. These platforms focus on flexible work opportunities and provide a wide range of job categories.

Job Boards for Remote and Hybrid Work:

1. **We Work Remotely**: One of the largest platforms dedicated to remote work opportunities across various industries. It offers a variety of job listings, from programming and design to marketing and customer service.

2. **Remote.co**: A resource hub that connects remote workers with companies offering remote positions. It also provides helpful advice for those looking to build a remote career.

3. **FlexJobs**: Offers a curated list of flexible job opportunities, including remote, freelance, and part-time positions. This platform ensures that all job listings are legitimate and vetted.

4. **AngelList**: Focuses on startups and technology companies, providing remote work opportunities for those with technical and creative skills.

5. **Jobspresso**: A high-quality job board for remote jobs in fields like marketing, programming, and customer support.

6. **Remotive**: Offers a collection of remote jobs in a wide range of industries, including tech, design, and customer support.

Remote Work Tools and Platforms:

1. **Slack**: A communication tool that helps remote teams stay connected. It's widely used for team collaboration, direct messaging, and file sharing.

2. **Trello**: A project management tool that organizes tasks and workflows, making it easy for remote teams to collaborate and stay on track.

3. **Zoom**: A video conferencing tool that has become essential for remote meetings, virtual conferences, and interviews.

4. **Asana**: A project management platform designed to help teams manage their tasks, deadlines, and projects efficiently, whether they're remote or hybrid.

5. **Notion**: An all-in-one workspace that combines notes, tasks, wikis, and databases, which is highly beneficial for remote workers who need to stay organized.

6. **Time Doctor**: A productivity tracking tool that helps remote workers manage their time efficiently, providing insights into how much time is spent on different tasks.

7. **GitHub**: For remote developers, GitHub is an essential platform for managing and collaborating on code. It's a version control system used globally by developers.

H2: Recommended Books and Courses

Continuous learning is a must for remote and hybrid workers to stay competitive in the ever-changing workplace. Below are some highly recommended books and courses that provide valuable insights into working remotely, managing a hybrid team, and enhancing your career skills.

Books:

1. **"Remote: Office Not Required" by Jason Fried and David Heinemeier Hansson**
   This book discusses the benefits of remote work and offers practical advice for both employees and employers. It highlights the importance of autonomy, trust, and communication in the remote work environment.

2. **"The Remote Work Handbook" by Global Workplace Analytics**
   This comprehensive guide outlines best practices for remote work, addressing everything from setting up a home office to navigating communication challenges.

3. **"The 4-Hour Workweek" by Timothy Ferriss**
   Although it's not exclusively about remote work, Ferriss's book offers powerful insights on productivity, time management, and the ability to design your own lifestyle—principles that are vital for remote workers.

4. **"Work Without Walls" by Maura Thomas**
   A fantastic read that explores strategies for maximizing productivity and maintaining balance while working remotely.

Courses:

1. **Remote Work Mastery on Udemy**
   This course covers everything you need to know about excelling in a remote work environment, from communication to time management. It's an excellent resource for those new to remote work.

2. **LinkedIn Learning – Time Management for Remote Workers**
   A course focused on helping remote workers stay productive and organized, offering tips and tools for managing time effectively.

3. **Coursera – Successful Remote Work**
   A course that covers the basics of working remotely, including how to communicate, collaborate, and maintain work-life balance while being productive.

4. **Skillshare – Remote Work Essentials**
   This course offers practical advice on tools, workflows, and strategies for succeeding in a hybrid or remote job. It also covers topics like team collaboration and building strong remote relationships.

H1: Sample Templates

Templates are great tools to streamline processes and reduce the time spent on administrative tasks. Below are two sample templates that are commonly used in remote work situations: a remote work cover letter and a productivity schedule example.

H2: Remote Work Cover Letter

A cover letter tailored to remote work should emphasize your self-discipline, adaptability, and ability to work independently. Here's a template you can use:

[Your Name]
[Your Address]
[City, State, Zip]
[Email Address]
[Phone Number]
[Date]

[Hiring Manager's Name]
[Company Name]
[Company Address]
[City, State, Zip]

Dear [Hiring Manager's Name],

I am writing to express my interest in the [Job Title] position at [Company Name], as advertised on [Platform/Website]. With [X] years of experience in [your field], I believe my skills in [relevant skills] and my ability to excel in a remote work environment make me a perfect candidate for this role.

Throughout my career, I have demonstrated the ability to manage projects independently, collaborate with remote teams, and consistently meet deadlines. I am highly proficient in remote communication tools such as Slack, Zoom, and Trello, and I am adept at managing my time and staying organized in a flexible work environment.

What excites me most about the opportunity at [Company Name] is your commitment to [mention something unique about the company]. I am confident that my passion for [industry/role] and my ability to work independently will allow me to make a significant contribution to your team.

Thank you for considering my application. I look forward to the possibility of discussing how my skills and experience align with your company's needs.

Sincerely,
[Your Name]

Sample 2

[Your Name]

 [Your Address]

[Your Phone Number]

[Your Email]

[Hiring Manager Name (if known)]

[Company Name]

 [Company Address]

Subject: Application for [Job Title] - [Your Name]

Dear [Mr./Ms./Mx. Hiring Manager Last Name],

I am writing to express my enthusiastic interest in the Remote [Job Title] position at [Company Name], as advertised on [Platform where you saw the job posting]. With my [Number] years of experience in [Relevant field] and proven success in remote work environments, I am confident I possess the skills and dedication to excel in this role and contribute significantly to your team's success.

In my previous role as [Your Previous Role] at [Your Previous Company], I consistently demonstrated my ability to:

- **[Quantifiable achievement 1, e.g., "Increase productivity by 15% while working remotely"]**
- **[Quantifiable achievement 2, e.g., "Successfully manage and deliver projects with geographically dispersed teams"]**
- **[Quantifiable achievement 3, e.g., "Proactively communicate and collaborate effectively in virtual settings"]**

I am a highly motivated and results-oriented individual with a strong work ethic. I thrive in independent environments while maintaining excellent communication and collaboration with colleagues. I am proficient in [List relevant software/tools, e.g., project management tools, communication platforms, video conferencing software] and possess a strong understanding of the challenges and rewards of remote work.

I am eager to contribute my skills and experience to a company that values innovation, flexibility, and employee well-being. I am confident that I can be a valuable asset to your remote team and am excited by the opportunity to contribute to [Company Name]'s continued success.

Thank you for your time and consideration. I have attached my resume for your review and welcome the opportunity to discuss my qualifications further in an interview.

Sincerely, [Your Name]

H2: Productivity Schedule Example

A productivity schedule helps remote workers stay organized and focused. Below is an example of a daily productivity schedule:

[Your Name]
Daily Productivity Schedule

6:00 AM – 7:00 AM: Morning Routine

- Meditation, stretching, breakfast.

7:00 AM – 9:00 AM: Deep Work Session

- Focused work on high-priority tasks (e.g., project work, writing, coding).

9:00 AM – 9:30 AM: Break

- Take a short walk or have a coffee.

9:30 AM – 12:00 PM: Collaboration Time

- Respond to emails, attend virtual meetings, team discussions.

12:00 PM – 1:00 PM: Lunch Break

- Disconnect from work to recharge.

1:00 PM – 3:00 PM: Deep Work Session

- Continue working on projects or tasks requiring focus.

3:00 PM – 3:30 PM: Break

- Stretch, relax, and rehydrate.

3:30 PM – 5:00 PM: Wrap Up and Planning for Tomorrow

- Complete remaining tasks, review progress, and organize the next day's agenda.

By utilizing these resources and templates, remote and hybrid workers can stay organized, improve productivity, and better manage their careers in the evolving landscape of work.